Legends of the Sea

PIRATES

Rebecca Rissman

Chicago, Illinois

www.heinemannraintree.com
Visit our website to find out more information about Heinemann-Raintree books.

To order:

☎ Phone 888-454-2279

🖳 Visit www.heinemannraintree.com to browse our catalog and order online.

©2010 Raintree
an imprint of Capstone Global Library, LLC
Chicago, Illinois

Edited by Rebecca Rissman, Nancy Dickmann, and Siân Smith
Designed by Joanna Hinton Malivoire and Ryan Frieson
Original illustrations ©Capstone Global Library 2010
Illustrated by Mendola Ltd
Picture research by Tracy Cummins
Production control by Victoria Fitzgerald
Originated by Capstone Global Library Ltd
Printed and bound in China by Leo Paper Products Ltd

14 13 12 11 10
10 9 8 7 6 5 4 3 2 1

Library of Congress Cataloging-in-Publication Data
Rissman, Rebecca.
Pirates / Rebecca Rissman. -- 1st ed.
p. cm. -- (Legends of the sea)
Includes bibliographical references and index.
ISBN 978-1-4109-3787-2 (hc)
ISBN 978-1-4109-3792-6 (pb)
1. Pirates--Juvenile literature. I. Title.
G535.R57 2011
910.4'5--dc22
             2009045462

Acknowledgments
The author and publishers are grateful to the following for permission to reproduce copyright material: akg-images p.**9**; AP Photo p.**15** (J. Pat Carter); Corbis pp.**17**, **19** (© Richard T. Nowitz); Getty Images p.**27** (Matthew Bash/U.S. Navy); istockphoto pp.**11** (© FrankCangelosi), **20** (© NoDerog); National Geographic p.**6** (Don Maitz); Shutterstock p.**27** (© Map Resources); The Art Archive p.**18** (Granger Collection); The Bridgeman Art Library International pp.**12** (Embleton, Ron (1930-88) / Private Collection / © Look and Learn), **13** (American School, (18th century) / Private Collection / Peter Newark Historical Pictures), **21** (English School, (19th century) / Private Collection / Peter Newark Historical Pictures), **22** (English School / Private Collection / Peter Newark Historical Pictures), **24** (American School, (18th century) / Private Collection / Peter Newark Historical Pictures), **25** (Private Collection / Peter Newark American Pictures); The Granger Collection, New York pp.**10**, **23**; The Kobal Collection p.**7** (Walt Disney).

Some words are shown in bold, **like this**. You can find out what they mean by looking in the glossary.

Contents

Is It True?

When it comes to pirates, some **legends**, or stories, seem too strange to be true. Can you guess if these legends are true or false?

All pirate ships flew a flag showing a skull and crossbones.

Blackbeard used to make people think he was on fire.

Pirates always buried their treasure.

Pirate ships weren't wild. In fact, they usually had a "Pirate **Code**," or list of rules they had to follow!

Read this book to find
out the answers!

Pirates

For as long as people have sailed the seas, there have been pirates. Pirates are sailors who attack other ships for money and power. Pirates have sailed all around the world.

This photo was taken from the film *Pirates of the Caribbean*.

Films about pirates are popular today. Filmmakers find out about pirates in the past to make their films more realistic.

Pirate Life

Believe it or not, a pirate's life wasn't all battles and war. Pirates spent most of their time at sea looking for their next **victims**. And life on a ship could get boring!

Pirate Code

Most pirates followed a **code**, or list of rules. Some pirate rules were:

- Lights out below **deck** at 8:00PM
- No fighting with each other
- Weapons must be kept clean and ready for use!

But when pirates spotted another ship, things could get very exciting!

Look Out—Pirate Attack!

Pirates flew a flag called the Jolly Roger to warn other ships that they were going to attack. This flag scared the sailors on other boats.

Jolly Roger

IS IT TRUE?

All pirate ships flew flags showing a skull and crossbones.

Answer: false. Some Jolly Roger flags were different designs and colors.

11

When pirates were ready to attack, they sailed next to another ship. Then one group of pirates would tie the two boats together while another group climbed across. Once pirates boarded their **victim's** ship, the fight really started!

grappling
hook

Tools of the Trade

Grappling Hooks: Pirates used these hooks to climb onto other ships.

Pirate Weapons

Once pirates boarded their **victim's** ship, they used weapons that helped them in **hand-to-hand** fighting. These included short knives and swords such as **daggers** and **cutlasses**. Pirates also used guns called **muskets** to kill their victims.

cutlass

musket

Pirates only used their cannons as a last resort. They didn't want to ruin the ships they were trying to steal!

Pirate Booty

Pirates didn't attack other ships just for fun—they were after **booty**, or treasure! Pirates also wanted to steal new ships.

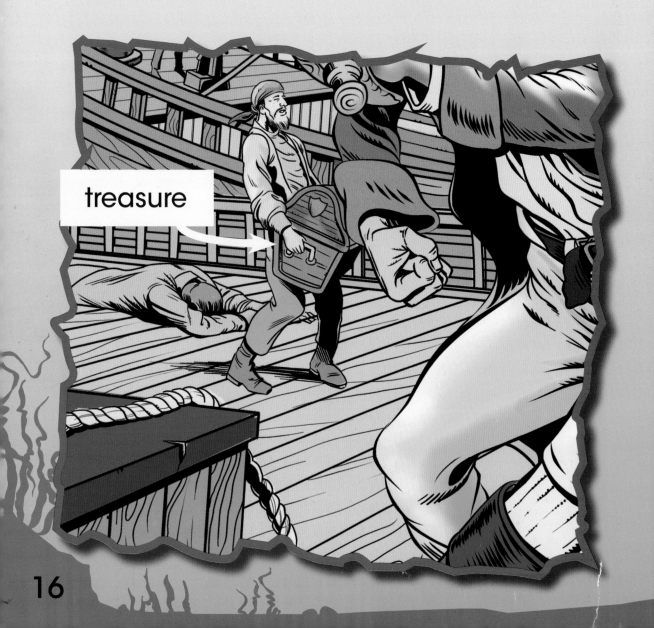

treasure

real pirate treasure

DID YOU KNOW?
Pirate treasure wasn't just gold and silver. Sometimes pirates took live treasure with them! Holding people **ransom** was a quick way to earn money.

Most of the time, pirates spent their treasure as fast as they could get it. But sometimes they stole so much treasure that they couldn't spend it all at once. Some pirates buried their treasure to keep it safe.

treasure

treasure

This pirate treasure was found at the bottom of the sea.

Famous Pirates

Blackbeard was one of the most famous pirates that ever lived. While he was a pirate, Blackbeard stole from over 40 ships.

15c

Blackbeard is so famous he has appeared on stamps!

IS IT TRUE?

To scare his **victims**, Blackbeard would light strips of cloth and tuck them into his beard. This made him look like he was on fire!

Answer: true

Black Bart

Black Bart was a very skilled pirate. **Legends** say that Black Bart stole 400 ships in just four years!

Another famous pirate was called Calico Jack. He was well known for his brightly colored clothing and for allowing women to join his **crew**.

Calico Jack

Not all famous pirates were men. Two of the fiercest pirates were women. Anne Bonny and Mary Read were pirates who attacked ships and stole treasure.

Anne and Mary dressed in men's clothing. Many of their **victims** had no idea they were women!

Pirates Today

There are still pirates around today. In fact, pirates rob hundreds of ships each year.

Key
X pirate attack

This map shows where the most pirate attacks occurred in 2009.

These modern pirates were captured near Somalia, in Africa.

Police and soldiers from around the world work together to keep people safe from pirates.

Talk Like a Pirate

Pirates sometimes used their own words to describe things on their ships. Can you guess which word matches with each part of the picture?

Crow's-nest

Figurehead

Helm

Poop deck

Glossary

booty stolen treasure. Pirate booty could include gold and jewels.

code list of rules pirates followed. Pirates followed different codes.

crew a group of people who work on and run a ship

cutlass curved sword

dagger short, pointed sword similar to a knife

deck area on a boat that people could walk on. Most decks are open to the air.

hand-to-hand close style of fighting

legend story that started long ago

musket old type of gun

ransom a trade of money or other payment asked in return for a person

victim person who is tricked or harmed

Find Out More

Books

John Matthews, *Pirates*, Carlton Books Ltd, 2009.

Mary Pope Osborne and Sal Murdocca, *Magic Tree House Research Guide: Pirates*, Random House Books for Young Readers, 2001.

Richard Platt, *DK Eyewitness Books: Pirate*, DK Publishing, 2007.

Websites

www.britishcouncil.org/kids-topics-pirates.htm
Test your knowledge of pirates with the pirate quiz on this website.

www.nationalgeographic.com/pirates/index.html
Play the "high seas adventure" to find out about famous pirates, ships, treasure, and more. Click on "Blackbeard" for the story behind this famous pirate.

www.thepirateking.com/index.htm
This website is packed with information on pirates including pirate weapons and pirate songs. Click on "Sailing Simulator" to try steering a pirate ship.

Find out

What type of weapon was the buckler?

Index